If you desire to grow a deeper understanding of true worship, then this book *Back to the Heart of Worship: Rediscovering the Reality of Authentic Worship* by Lawrence Salley II is what you need to catapult you into the deep. Lawrence describes the many different aspects of worship and the proper way to devote yourself as you reverence our Heavenly Father. This book is a skillfully written, well thought out masterpiece.

I highly recommend this book; it is a must-read for every believer.

-Khalilah Velez, Author of Growing in Christ

Compelling and Practical! Lawrence provides an excellent foundation on the importance of worship. He imparts intriguing worship principles that will surely ignite you. I am confident that as he unpacks the meaning of worship you will discover a renewed passion and purpose.

-Prophet Marcus Allen, Your Prophetic Coach

Back to the Heart of Worship

Back to the Heart of Worship
By Lawrence Salley II

Back to the Heart of Worship: Rediscovering the Reality of Authentic Worship
Published by Lawrence Salley Ministries

WWW.LSMReal.com

International Standard Booking Number – 979-8-64922-838-1
Library of Congress Control Number: 2020909901

Copyright © 2020 by Lawrence Salley II

Scripture quotations marked by AMP are taken from the Amplified® Bible (AMP), Copyright © 2015 by The Lockman Foundation Used by permission. WWW.LOCKMAN.ORG

Scripture quotations marked NLT are taken from the Holy Bible, New Living Translation, copyright © 1996, 2004, 2015 by Tyndale House Foundation. Used by permission of Tyndale House Publishers, Inc., Carol Stream, Illinois 60188. All rights reserved.

Scripture quotations marked KJV are from the King James Version of the Bible.

Printed by Kingdom Direct Publishing (KDP), in the United States of America. First Edition, 2020

Cover design by L. Salley Blueprints, lsalleybluerints@gmail.com

Visit the Author's website at
www.LSMReal.com

DEDICATION

The spiritual assignment of this book is to all worship leaders, both psalmists and minstrels, who have committed to creating atmospheres for God-shifting movements.

CONTENTS

ACKNOWLEDGEMENTS

To my wife, Airlia Salley and daughter, Jaidyn Nicole Salley. You two have been my inspiration from day one. You have encouraged me during my low seasons and celebrated my high seasons. You have tolerated my long nights in front of the computer. You pulled me to the front when I became lost in my own world. You kept me balance through it all.

To my grandparents, Apostle Laiton and Prophetess Barbara Bailey and the entire Upon This Rock family. You all have taught me the meaning of a strong and solid foundation and the value and family and connection. You have birthed the skills of a leader, teacher and student in me. Because of your seed, I can stand on what I truly believe from God even when others don't agree. You have taught me that the Word of God is the best thing that I have and will not change.

To Doctors Apostle Precious and Prophet Carolyn Ewuzie and the New Gate Church Int'l family. You have taught me the advanced principles of intercession and provided a place for training and development in worship and warfare.

To Pastors Ralph and Shay Holmes and the Redeemers House of Worship family. Thank you for walking me through the doors of leadership and releasing me into my greater! I no longer have to dream about my "next" for you have brought me to my "now"!

To all my family and friends who have prayed with me, encouraged me, sowed the Word into me and have kept me on my toes. I pray God's blessing upon you!

Additional coaches and influencers who have provided Godly wisdom and counsel for healing and growth:

Pastor Karen Jethroe

Dr. Alexis McClinton

Prophet Marcus Allen

Apostle Paula Covington-Shelby

Prophetess Lucretia Lewis

Pastor Donzell Snipes

Evangelist Marie Sally

Brenda Bailey

Pastor Laiton Deandre Bailey

The Sterlings Family

Pastor Theron Armstead & Lady Ursula Armstead

Darnell Baldwin

Jason Lemons

Frances Price

Jennifer Williams

Ella Marisha Camp

Khalilah Velez

Arasele Nazario

<u>Rediscovering the Reality of Authentic Worship</u>

FOREWORD

Books almost without number have been written on Worship. This undertaking by Lawrence Salley can be elusive, depends on many factors, and is dependent on spiritual forces that lie beyond the control of the worshipper. Worship must have Worshipper's born from above and driven by the wind of the Spirit. The trumpet must sound; otherwise the troops will not assemble for battle. We need clear words, clarion calls, and specific strategies from the Lord! Thankfully God is raising up Worshippers in this generation, and the gift of worship is being released afresh throughout the Body around the world. One such Worshipper is Lawrence. That is wonderful news to me; that is Good News!

The Bible is clear that God demands to be worshipped for who He truly is. No one can honor the Father unless the Son is honored; likewise, it is impossible to honor the Father and the Son while dishonoring the Spirit. Yet every day many offer praises to a patently false image of Holy Spirit. They have become like the Israelites of

Exodus 32, who compelled Aaron to fashion a golden calf while Moses was away.

Worshipping depends so much on the spiritual state of the worshipper; the spiritual state of the congregation; the ripeness and readiness of a God-related idea; and other considerations as well. Lawrence has extended a challenge for us all "we must take time to understand the standard of what God receives as worship." I took the challenge personally to crucify myself as I studied the pages of this important manual. I was encouraged to believe God for a greater manifestation of the Spirit of Worship in my own life and service. All in all I found Back to the Heart of Worship a rich reading experience. And when I came to Chapter 4; "Why Worship" I felt faith rising within me, and I was ready to worship Him in the beauty of His Holiness.

If you listen to God and have felt the "temperature" of the Spirit realm steadily rise, this book will confirm to you what He has spoken to us about Worship. As you read, God will deposit something "new" inside of you if you ask for it. Receive and embrace this Word. Receive this prophetic call, and God will bless, strengthen, and guide you in your worship experiences. Your heart will begin to turn in a new direction...and, like me/us you will know that you can never turn back.

Well done *Son-Son*. Pastor Shay and I are proud of you!

Pastors Ralph & Shay Holmes

Pastors of Redeemers House of Worship – Belleville, IL

INTRODUCTION

There is a thought that says, "No one can teach you how to worship because it is personal between you and God." I must say there is some truth to this statement; however, I dare to challenge a specific point of this thought. Indeed, we cannot teach the essence of worship. Worship is embedded into the image of man. It is a natural function. No one taught you how to respond to the moment when your heart was captured and drawn to something; it was never a fight to surrender and you never questioned the agenda. I would stretch to voice, there was no second-guessing the motive or intent of what or to whom you were attracted. It was one hundred percent free-will.

What am I challenging? Everything I mentioned argues your worship is indeed personal. I believe, even though humanity is embedded with the natural ability to worship, we must take time to understand the standard of what God receives as worship. Once we align our signal with God's frequency, we expose ourselves to a lifestyle of miracles, signs and wonders.

Present Yourself...

Let us dive into this matter even further. The phrase "present yourself" is mentioned only 4 times through the bible. Yet I believe it carries much more significance. When we read or hear that phrase, we understand there is a call to order. Looking at it from a conventional perspective, the one class most young adults love the least is speech class, where the level of presenting carries much weight.

Students are not expected to get up and start babbling about the first thing that comes to mind. There is a process. Topics are assigned within an expectation of carrying out an in-depth study. The class is accountable for acquiring raw data, new information and familiar knowledge, somehow creating a structure that allows their audience to follow. After gathering information, the student realizes that information alone can convince the audience, but not capture the same.

Through this experience, I have discovered one of the greatest secrets to executing a successful speech: knowing your audience. During the preparation process, an "attention-getter" needs to be in place - something that displays passion and personal interest. When we skillfully connect our passion with the passion of our audience, the capture becomes successful. During the speech, the audience is compelled to cry, laugh, experience suspense and overall connect to your speech emotionally. If this is relayed effectively, you have presented yourself.

What you are about to indulge in was birthed through this very thought, that we must know what pleases the Father when it comes to worship. How do we glorify the Father in the things we do? I want to visit three dimensions of the word "present" that will enhance our understanding of worship: Establish. Approach, Sacrifice.

Chapter 1

YATSAG - ESTABLISH

This word is Hebrew for "set, put, and establish." David demonstrated yatsag when he and his army "presented" the ark of the covenant in the middle of the tabernacle or tent that he dedicated for worship. Whatever is presented is on display and not hidden. That indicates intentionality.

> *And they brought in the ark of the LORD and set it in its place, inside the tent that David had pitched for it. And David offered burnt offerings and peace offerings before the LORD.*
>
> *2 Samuel 6:17*

And they brought in the ark of God and set it inside the tent that David had pitched for it, and they offered burnt

*offerings and peace offerings before God. 1 Chronicles
16:1*

Everything we do is on display. Whether we do it for ungodly motives or we do to please God, what we display outwardly reflects what we establish inwardly. It is impossible to please God and man at the same time.

> *God's purpose in all this was to use the church to display his wisdom in its rich variety to all the unseen rulers and authorities in the heavenly places.*
>
> *Ephesians 3:10 NLT*

Many times during worship, I have found myself stuck in a place of insecurity because my focus was on the wrong person. Frequently, we consider worship as "ministering to the congregation." With this concept in mind, we find ourselves battling with the thought of keeping smiles on people's faces. Being the worship leader at various churches, I thought that I was doing the right thing by taking in every feedback given from everyone. What I was doing was catering to the wrong audience.

We must always be teachable; however, a line can be crossed. My thoughts were consumed with the wrong questions. "Will this please my leaders?" or "Should I impress my leaders by doing this?" Don't get it twisted. I believe communication should be established when it comes to understanding the seasons of the ministry, so we are on one accord. The agreement should center around what God is doing , not what we feel or desire. With that being said, my question should always remain as "Will this please God?" The beauty of serving God is we don't have to try to impress Him. In truth, the only way to impress God is when we function in faith.

When we display God, He displays much more for us! Putting God on display in our lives and during our worship services creates space for God to shine. God is, sure enough sovereign; therefore, He can do what He pleases. How much more would God do for us when we willfully create space for Him. When we create space for God, He creates space for His glory, power, signs, holiness, and more!

The LORD replied, "Listen, I am making a covenant with you in the presence of all your people. I will perform miracles that have never been performed anywhere in all the earth or in any nation. And all the people around you will see the power of the LORD - the awesome power I will display for you."

Exodus 34:10 NLT

*Summon your might, O God. Display your power, O God,
as you have in the past.*

Psalm 68:28 NLT

Another benefit of establishing God as our audience is that He settles us in return. The more we put God in display, the more He stabilizes us. As long as Israel displayed God and established God as their King, the more God secured them from their enemies; he secured their resources and wealth; he secured their safety. Every aspect of Israel was secured. The moment they swayed away from God was the moment they lost their sense of security. God never left them, but they suffered significant losses. To be placed in right standing with God, they had to perform sacrifices for the atonement of their sins.

When we establish God as our audience, we begin to glorify His Son. Honoring Christ in our lives establishes God as our Father. The sacrifice of Jesus paid the ransom for our sins. That is very important because it takes us away from "dead works" into a lifestyle of grace. What we do is never to make ourselves right before God, but it is all expressions of faith. The revelation of faith is excellent news for us. That means, when we establish Christ as our LORD and Savior, God establishes us in Christ. Our safety, security, success, and resources are secured in Christ. God is stabilizing us!

Something stable is something that does not move or break. When something is stable, there is security with no loose ends. Consider the children of Israel. They were God's chosen people, and His prized possession, nonetheless, unstable. They honored God for short lengths of time, sequenced by falling subject to foreign gods and idols. They were in and out of captivity due to the inconsistency of obedience.

Christ plants us! God knows we cannot consistently do right because we are unaware of all the thoughts and feelings in our hearts. But when we keep our eyes on someone consistent - Christ - it allows God to transform us into His image. No matter the mistakes we make in life, or the times we misread God, our covenant with God never breaks because of Christ. The more we yield to God, the more God plants us. Even though we cannot live a perfect life, we can make conscious efforts to stay near God.

Chapter 2

QARAB - APPROACH

The equivalent meanings of this word are "offer, come or draw near, and approach." Learning to present yourself before God is about understanding the ability to approach and draw near to God. The scripture reminds us that God will draw closer to us as we draw closer to him. Presenting yourself to God is when we display divine interest in the desires of God. In the following scripture, we see "the chosen" is defined by those who draw near to God.

Blessed (happy, fortunate, to be envied) is the man whom You choose and cause to come near, that he may dwell in Your courts! We shall be satisfied with the goodness of Your house, Your holy temple.

Psalm 65:4 AMPC

This illuminates a deeper understanding of the scriptures "many are called but few are chosen." (Matthew 20:16) God invites many to fellowship with Him but it takes submission to draw back to God.

I find it interesting that God always makes the first move, yet we live in a society that teaches us that we must move first. Whether it is making provision for us before we see it, or initiating a shift by speaking, God always makes the first move, though you do not regularly see it.

When we draw near to God, it is not because we have found a sudden interest in God. It is because He has chosen to come near to us. That may sound petty but think about it. How awesome is it to pursue a God who pursues you first?

We see this same principle in marriage. The Bible describes the church as a woman or bride, and Christ as the groom. We see this great marriage birthed through the finished works of the Cross. As we dig deeper, we find that it is the responsibility of the groom to find the wife. The function of the groom is a powerful illustration that shows the pursuit of Christ for us - the Church. Though something is first, does not mean the weight of it is always more substantial. Yes, there is immense significance, but in this case, to be sought out first is as important as our response.

I want to go further into the word "find." There is so much to unpack in this word. We are used to the surface meaning of the word, seek or uncover. Maybe you are more familiar with defining the word "find" with "to discover." The Hebrew word "find" translates to secure, to be sufficient, and to be enough. Another meaning for find is "to be left after the war." When I consider these definitions to define one word, I think of a vigorous pursuit. God didn't accidentally come across us. He intentionally sought after us and fought for us! He is our creator!

You are sufficient for God to initiate a search warrant for your soul. You were enough to seek after. Romans reminds us that those He predestined, He also called, those He called, He also justified; and those he justified, he also glorified. God knew what He was doing when He chased after you.

> *And those whom he predestined he also called, and those whom he called he also justified, and those whom he justified he also glorified.*
>
> *Romans 8:30*

Have considered the fight that Christ endured in pursuit of you? From the beating at the whipping post to the carrying of the Cross. From the mocking of the crown to the piercing on the side. Christ took on deliberate war to ensure the salvation of our souls. We have guaranteed access to the Father all because of the finished work of

Christ. We are the prize for His endurance. As a result of His ascension to Heaven, we are those who remain on the earth as active ambassadors of Christ and his beneficiaries of His kingdom.

15

Chapter 3

MINCHAH - SACRIFICE

The third variation of the word "present" is pronounced min-khä. The meaning of this Hebrew word is gift, offering, and sacrifice. I believe it is quite clear that this Hebrew word can effortlessly identify worship. We can undeniably see worship ties to all three and much more, but when we think of worship, we often think of this variation.

> *Ascribe to the LORD the glory that is due his name; bring*
> *an offering and come into his courts!*
>
> *Psalm 96:8*

It is essential to recognize that we are not owners but merely stewards. We are stewards of our bodies. We are stewards of our gifts. What we have does not belong to us, not even the breath in our bodies. Everything that surrounds us or is associated with us eventually goes back to the One who created it all.

The earth is the LORD's and the fullness thereof, the world and those who dwell therein.

Psalm 24:1

Worship, as we know, requires action from the start - the awakening, the relating, and the returning. The offering of a gift is a returning act. We are naturally giving God what he has given to us! How far are we willing to go? How much are we willing to give up?

Let us take a look at history. Abraham was promised to be the father of nations! The uncountable stars would represent the number of children he would have. The counting of the sand would also symbolize the insurmountable increase of his children. Although there were a few obstacles they faced, God yet fulfilled His promise to Abraham. As we fast forward, we understand that God required a sacrifice from Abraham. That was an inconceivable sacrifice because we knew there was no bull or lamb at that particular time that would serve as the sacrifice.

After years of hoping and believing God for this miracle, Abraham was asked to fulfill one of the most challenging tasks of sacrificing his son as an act of giving back to God what God gave to him. Right at the nick of time, a ram appeared in the bush. The ram replaced Isaac as the sacrifice. God's response to the task was as follows:

By myself I have sworn, declares the LORD, because you have done this and have not withheld your son, your only son, I will surely bless you, and I will surely multiply your offspring as the stars of heaven and as the sand that is on the seashore. And your offspring shall possess the gate of their enemies, and your offspring shall all the nations of the earth be blessed because you have obeyed my voice.

Genesis 22:15-18

Another story I love reading about is Samuel's mother, Hannah - a barren woman who was taunted by the second wife of Elkanah, Peninnah. Isn't it amazing how our gifts are birthed through agony? After the final straw, Hannah prayed God would bless her with a son. In return, she would dedicate her son back to Him. Sometimes we live with unanswered prayers because we have no intention of giving God glory or honor with what we've requested.

God heard Hannah's prayer and blessed her with Samuel. Committed to her word, Hannah dedicated her son to the temple. As a response to her sacrifice, Samuel was the first of many children birthed through Hannah. Offering our gifts back to God activates a "first of many" anointing as we saw it with Abraham and Isaac, Hannah and Samuel, and even God and Christ.

The man Elkanah and all his house went up to offer to the LORD the yearly sacrifice and to pay his vow. But Hannah did not go up, for she said to her husband, "As soon as the child is weaned, I will bring him, so that he will appear in the presence of the LORD and dwell there forever." Elkanah her husband said to her, "Do what seems best to you; wait until you have weaned him; only, may the LORD establish his word." So the woman remained and nursed her son until she weaned him. And when she had weaned him, she took him up with her, along with a three-year-old bull, an ephah of flour, and a skin of wine, and she brought him to the house of the LORD at Shiloh. And the child was young. Then they slaughtered the bull, and they brought the child to Eli. And she said, "Oh, my lord! As you live, my lord, I am the woman who was standing here in your presence, praying to the LORD. For this child I have prayed, and the LORD granted me my petition that I made to him. Therefore I have lent him to the LORD. As long as he lives, he is lent to the LORD."

1 Samuel 1:21-28

Indeed the LORD visited Hannah, and she conceived and bore three sons and two daughters. And the boy Samuel grew in the presence of the LORD. And he worshipped the LORD there.

1 Samuel 2:21

But in fact, Christ has been raised from the dead, the first fruits of those who have fallen asleep. For as by a man came death, by a man has come also the resurrection of the dead. For as in Adam all die, so also in Christ shall all be made alive. But each in his own order: Christ the first fruits, then at his coming those who belong to Christ.

1 Corinthians 15:20-23

God loves to multiply what we give him. There was a saying that I grew up hearing: "you can't out-give God!" God always finds ways to provide us with more than we can imagine or think. It is His nature, but He cannot multiply what we are not willing to release to him.

When we look at the word "present," we now see there is an establishment that takes place. You establish your audience. You establish the One you are pleasing. Once you establish the Who, you then draw near to that Who. Jesus is our Lord and Savior. Revelation invites us to worship Christ. (Revelation 19:10) You then draw near to

Christ. The more you draw near to Christ, the more He will reveal Himself to you. You begin to know the likes and dislikes of God. The loves and hates of God are embedded in your heart. Now it is time we offer our gifts and sacrifices to God.

The order of Worship: Establish, Approach, and Sacrifice.

Therefore, I urge you, brothers and sisters, by the mercies of God, to present your bodies [dedicating all of yourselves, set apart] as a living sacrifice, holy and well-pleasing to God, which is your rational (logical, intelligent) act of worship.

Romans 12:1 AMP

22

Chapter 4

WHY WORSHIP

Over the years the culture of the church has changed significantly. We have evolved from heavy choir robes to stage lights and fog machines. We have transitioned from singing hymnals accompanied by an organ or out of tune piano to acoustic guitars and other string instruments. We have encountered several movements from the Evangelical movement to the Charismatic shifts. We've matured from segregated congregations to mixed assemblies of worship. Our worship in itself has changed.

Have we advanced in our worship as a body or have we drifted away from its simplicity? Our worship to God is a form of submission, compared to a husband and wife. To honor means to submit and to respect. We are not only acknowledging that we need God, but we come to the revelation that God also desires us. Our beauty is supposed to attract the very presence of God. Psalms 96:6 states we ought to worship the Lord in the beauty of holiness. We cannot come before God anyway. Coming to worship is not the same as coming to salvation. Just as David did, we must also learn to remove layers of filth before we come before the presence of God in worship.

And the king will desire your beauty. Since he is your lord, bow to him.

Psalm 45:11

O come, let us worship and bow down; let us kneel before the LORD, our Maker!

Psalm 95:6

Worship the LORD in the splendor of holiness; tremble before him, all the earth!

Psalm 96:9

Then David arose from the earth and washed and anointed himself and changed his clothes. And he went into the house of the LORD and worshiped. He then went

to his own house. And when he asked, they set food
before him, and he ate.

2 Samuel 12:20

There is only one worship, but there are two dimensions: the lifestyle of worship and the expressions of worship.

Obedience

Through obedience is how we accomplish the lifestyle of worship. That is when we present ourselves living sacrifices, living holy and acceptable lives. When we offer ourselves as living sacrifices, we live through obedience, not giving God dead works. God seeks obedience above sacrifice. This worship is when we have total compliance with the plans of God for our lives. Through this, Genesis and Romans are birthed: proper dominion is restored, and the manifestation of the Sons of God arise within us.

God pays attention to the condition of the heart above appearance, and He values obedience more than sacrifices. Obedience stems from the heart! Samuel and David were a couple of the first individuals that understood God did not delight in blood sacrifices, but a life of obedience was God's desire from His people.

*For you will not delight in sacrifice, or I would give it; you
will not be pleased with a burnt offering.*

Psalm 51:16

*"What to me is the multitude of your sacrifices? says the
LORD; I have had enough of burnt offerings of rams and
the fat of well-fed beasts; I do not delight in the blood of
bulls, or of lambs, or of goats."*

Isaiah 1:11

Partial Obedience is Disobedience

Saul was given instructions to destroy everything in a particular
battle, but he chose to withhold some for the sake of a sacrifice to
God. Oftentimes, God gives us instructions, but we hold back on
executing them for the purpose of keeping peace or fear. Regardless of
the reason, God knew what you would come against, yet the
instructions were given. My question to you is, when did God become
more concerned about sacrifice than obedience? God taught us
through Saul, partial obedience is disobedience regardless of the
reason, it is still disobedience. Stay obedient to God and fight fear
with Faith!

And Samuel said, "Has the LORD as great delight in burnt offerings and sacrifices, as in obeying the voice of the LORD? Behold, to obey is better than sacrifice, and to listen than the fat of rams. For rebellion is as the sin of divination, and presumption is as iniquity and idolatry. Because you have rejected the world of the LORD, he has also rejected you from being king."

1 Samuel 15:22-23

When we submit ourselves to the obedience of God, we begin to experience a glory like never before. This glory is more than a Sunday experience. This glory encounter pushes us from being the tail and carries us to the head, it takes us from being below and places us above. Deuteronomy 28:1-13 gives us details of what obedience does for us. It illustrates worship in lifestyle form. Those who are obedient to God are entitled to the blessings.

- ✓ Blessed in the City and in the Field
- ✓ Fruit of your womb, the fruit of your ground and the fruit of your cattle shall be blessed and bring forth increase
- ✓ Your basket and your kneading bowl shall be blessed
- ✓ Blessed when you come in, and when you go out

- ✓ Your enemies who rise against you shall be defeated before you. When they came out against you, they flee before you seven ways
- ✓ Your barns and all that you undertake will be blessed. He will bless the land that He gives you
- ✓ You are established as a people holy to God
- ✓ All the people of the earth shall see that you are called by the name of the LORD
- ✓ You will abound in prosperity, the fruit of your womb, the fruit of your livestock and the fruit of your ground
- ✓ The treasures of heaven are open to you, providing rain to your land in its season and bless all the work of your hands
- ✓ You will lend to many nations but will not borrow
- ✓ You will be made the head and not the tail
- ✓ You shall go up and not down

In summary, when we yield to Holy Spirit, blessings are literally all around us and in everything we do. The more I read the bible, the more I am convinced that we have no actual contribution to our success, other than obedience. That is good news because leaving the fate of our success in the hands of God can lead to nothing but greatness. Age, experience, talents or gifting does not validate your ability to participate in success - obedience does!

The remaining of this book focuses on the second realm of worship - the manifestation of the glory of God through our expressions. When we express our gratitude and love for God through song, dance, and instruments, it causes the glory of God to manifest around us. That is also a lifestyle, but it focuses on an intentional encounter with God. This realm of worship is subsequent to your obedience to God.

Chapter 5

SOLID FOUNDATION

I have discovered four elements of what makes our worship effective and stronger: Love, Faith, the Word of God, and the Spirit of God. When we take the time to build ourselves through these areas, what we do becomes stronger and creates a heavier impact on our fellowship with God and our influence with others.

Love

The bottom line is without love, nothing we do has value. Love deals with our obedience to God. The bible tells us directly that we must learn to love God as well as our neighbors. Love is the principle of sacrifice. We have discussed in detail our sacrifice to God is our livelihood. Exchanging our desires and plans for the obedience of God. 1 Corinthians 13, also known as the Love Chapter, details our love for each other, how we interact with each other, and how we respond to the flaws of each other.

Hatred stirs up strife, but love covers all offenses.

Proverbs 10:12

Above all, keep loving one another earnestly, since love covers a multitude of sins.

1 Peter 4:8

Without love there would be no access to eternal life.

For God so loved the world, that he gave his only Son, that whoever believes in him should not perish but have eternal life.

John 3:16

Love is so important that the bibles tells us to put aside every gift, every talent, every assignment until we get it right with each other.

So if you are offering your gift at the altar and there remember that your brother has something against you, leave your gift there before the altar and go. First be reconciled to your brother, and then come and offer your gift.

Matthew 5:23-24

Without love, we cannot truly live in obedience. That alone disqualifies us from partaking in worship. Jesus spoke of this plainly in John 13.

> *"A new commandment I give to you, that you love one another: just as I have loved you, you also are to love one another. By this all people will know that you are my disciples, if you have love for one another."*

John 13:34-35

Love is our response to people who mistreat us. Love is our response to people who turn their backs on us. Love is the response to people who disagree with us. Love is the response to people who even speak curses upon us because love is what separates us from those who dwell in darkness.

Have you ever heard an unorganized or dysfunctional orchestra? It sounds very similar to the warm-up session right before the musical is performed, neglecting rhythm, melody, order, and structure. Everyone is on separate timing. Different parts of the song and maybe even different scores are played at the same time. Do you get the picture? That is how we sound and appear without love.

Love is not seasonal and there is never a moment where love is not involved. Prophecy has an expiration date or a moment of fulfillment. Tongues come and go. Knowledge can be broken and never received whole. Love will be the same throughout it all. Love is so pure, its definition does not change based on the season, circumstance or environment. Love carries its own value and is non-dependent on any external force. In stretch, love is a realm that causes everything around to confo rm to it. Love keeps the foundation strong. Love provides the whole picture. Love matures us.

Love never ends. As for prophecies, they will pass away; as for tongues, they will cease; as for knowledge, it will pass away. For we know in part and we prophesy in part, but when the perfect comes, the partial will pass away. When I was a child, I spoke like a child, I thought like a child, I reasoned like a child. When I became a man, I gave up childish ways. For now we see in a mirror dimly, but then face to face. Now I know in part; then I shall know fully, even as I have been fully known. So now faith, hope, and love abide, these three; but the greatest of these is love.

1 Corinthians 13:8-13

Faith

Everything that we do requires faith! The bible tells us that without faith, it is impossible to please God. We cannot accept salvation without faith; we cannot receive healing or deliverance without faith. Without faith, we cannot obtain the promises of God. We cannot walk in purpose without faith. We cannot prophesy without faith. Essentially, we cannot worship God without faith.

And without faith it is impossible to please him, for whoever would draw near to God must believe that he exists and that he rewards those who seek him.

Hebrews 11:6

Having gifts that differ according to the grace given to us, let us use them: if prophecy, in proportion to our faith;

Romans 12:6

Our response to obeying God as well as participating in expressive acts of gratitude and thanksgiving - singing, dancing and instruments - equates to a level of works, partnered with our faith. Faith without works is dead, and to worship God without the proper faith is comparable to Cain presenting an offering to God with something that God cursed - it was dead!

> *For as the body apart from the spirit is dead, so also faith apart from works is dead.*
>
> *James 2:26*

Similar to love, everything we do requires faith. God's blueprint cannot be fulfilled without partnering with faith.

> *For in it the righteousness of God is revealed from faith for faith, as it is written, "The righteous shall live by faith."*
>
> *Romans 1:17*

I used to believe that our faith increases over time. The scripture above sheds a different light. Every man was given a measure of faith. Anything given to us by God comes whole and complete. Our faith does not come in levels. The scripture is saying the righteousness of God starts with faith and ends with faith. There is nothing wrong with your faith. It is up to us to learn what our measure is.

For by the grace given to me I say to everyone among you not to think of himself more highly than be ought to think, but to think with sober judgment, each according to the measure of faith that God has assigned.

Romans 12:3

The Word of God

The Word of God is crucial not just for our worship but for our daily living. When we intake fruit and vegetables, our natural body extracts all the nutrients and vitamins that contribute to the proper functioning of our body. We also know from childhood experiences that when we consume excessive junk and fast food, our bodies receive insufficient substances to fight against harmful bacteria and viruses that directly attack our immune system, digestive system, respiratory system, neurological system and more.

The Word of God is just as vital to our spiritual body as appropriate food is to our natural body. The Word of God gives us the necessary nutrients to fight against the bacteria and viruses Satan tries to place in our lives.

But he answered, "It is written, 'Man shall not live by bread alone, but by every word that comes from the mouth of God.'"

Matthew 4:4

And Jesus answered him, "It is written, 'Man shall not live by bread alone.'"

Luke 4:4

Now some of us are more visual learners. God gave us a live example of His word. The bible says that Jesus was the Word made into flesh. As we tap into the life of Christ, we begin to dig into a well of supply. Through revelation, we find that the Word of God is Christ, Himself - our mediator. He is the one who is continually making intercession for us. How mind-blowing is that? The Word of God is always fighting for us, but we must learn to use it. In other words, there is not one moment that the Word will not manifest in our favor or work on our behalf once we use it. The key is: we have to apply the word to our daily living.

The Word of God gives us access to our purpose, the will of God, the remedy to our lack, and opportunities for personal improvement.

And the Word became flesh and dwelt among us, and we have seen his glory, glory as of the only Son from the Father, full of grace and truth.

John 1:14

Who is to condemn? Christ Jesus is the one who died - more than that, who was raised - who is at the right hand of God, who indeed is interceding for us.

Romans 8:34

Worship points us to Christ! Worship causes us to see the Word of God in a new light.

Then I fell down at his feet to worship him, but he said to me, "You must not do that! I am a fellow servant with you and your brothers who hold to the testimony of Jesus. Worship God." For the testimony of Jesus is the spirit of prophecy.

Revelation 19:10

The Bible provides weaponry understanding, but praise and worship teaches us how to engage in warfare.

Heaven and earth will pass away, but my words will not pass away.

When we feed ourselves the Word of God daily, we enter into a realm of never-ending revelation, never-ending growth, and never-ending worship.

Spirit of God

There have been times in my life when I was consumed with knowing the bible in its entirety, believing it would help me understand more about worship, deliverance, kingdom and the prophetic. In the end, I felt tossed from left to right by the many variations people released. Now, however, my heart is balanced to know the Spirit of God. I forget from time to time the Spirit teaches, reveals and knows all things, even the deepest thoughts of God. Only the Spirit can bring us to a single mind.

Understand that the Spirit of God does not replace the Word of God. He makes the Word of God come to life. The basic requirements of worship are found in John: "For God is Spirit, so those who worship him must worship in spirit and in truth." We will dive further into this scripture in Chapter 7.

Holy Spirit also connects us to the senses of God. Many times we only associate the Holy Spirit to the voice of God, but the Holy Spirit also reminds us how close God truly is to His people. Holy Spirit is also known as the Spirit of Christ. Once we receive salvation, we inherit the Spirit of Christ, the Comforter, the Counselor, the Teacher, and this Spirit is on the inside of us!

You, however, are not in flesh but in the Spirit, if in fact the Spirit of God dwells in you. Anyone who does not have the Spirit of Christ does not belong to him.

Romans 8:9

I can recall a time when my family and I were transitioning out of a ministry. Before joining another local church, we underwent the process of healing and detoxing. My mentor instructed me to take some time to worship God with a unique purpose. The purpose was to discover the tangible side of God. Because of my position in ministry, I spent so much time pouring out to people, I never took time to allow God to pour into me. During that time, I realized God wanted to connect with me on an intimate level. He wanted me to know and feel His presence. The power of the Holy Spirit enabled me to experience another side of God.

God also brings clarity through the Holy Spirit during worship. I have learned to keep a pen and paper nearby when I am worshipping, whether I am praying or singing to God. I've experienced profound moments in God and the Holy Spirit was right there to release fresh wisdom and understanding concerning God's Word and complex situations in life.

For the LORD gives wisdom: from his mouth come knowledge and understanding;

Proverbs 2:6

For who knows a person's thoughts except the spirit of that person, which is in him? So also no one comprehends the thoughts of God except the Spirit of God. Now we have received not the spirit of the world, but the Spirit who is from God, that we might understand the things freely given us by God.

1 Corinthians 2:11-12

When we take love and our faith, and partner with the Word of God and the Spirit of God, it destroys the impossible ideology. As you go deeper into worship you walk into the reality that no rules apply. Thinking outside of the box becomes non-existent because your eyes become open to see that the box never existed.

43

Chapter 6

PROPER ORDER OF SERVICE

The Spirit of God is the Order of Service!

Many churches are not able to experience a consistent manifestation of the Presence of God because of the order of service. The Word of God can come through the realm of Worship. We must learn to wait on the Lord and allow His Glory to sir us. When evaluating the current condition of our churches and the lack of the Kabod experience, we must look at several assets of our churches to determine what is lacking in those areas.

The Worship Team

Many churches have adopted the concept of having a worship team. Looking back over the years, we can see, as mentioned earlier, there has been an evolving transition from the choir, to praise team, to worship team.

Choir >>> Praise Team >>> Worship Team

In some churches, as a way to capture both our new and older generation combined, we have merged the two to have both a choir and a few select singers who are singled out on individual microphones. Which one is most effective? The truth is there is no right answer because it depends on the hearts that are involved.

If they are all effective in ushering the glory of God, why are they not working at particular churches? One of the obvious reasons is that the method of worship could be outdated for the audience. You have a young crowd but singing older songs. Eventually, they get bored and either leave the church as a whole or leave that specific ministry once they are of age. By dwelling on older songs, we miss the opportunities discovering the mysteries of God through song. We limit God to our understanding and our boundaries.

We also deal with the ignorance of building a proper and effective worship team. I used to believe that the blueprint was hidden in the first mention of the Levitical Priesthood as songs and music were not always the image of expressive worship, as we know today.

My experience as a worship leader was to teach the do's and don'ts when it came to the theological side of worship. I was leading a team based on desperate tactics. We all knew there was a higher, more intimate atmosphere of worship that we were pursuing. My solution was knowledge-based. We must know! The approach I took was breaking down the Levitical duties of preparing the tabernacle.

From that teaching, it worked for a moment. Our conviction was renewed, and our worship was taken a bit higher. After a while, we once again reached a cap in our worship. What were we doing wrong? Why were we in these cycles of being stuck and not knowing what next to do?

The issue was we were using an old model method, hoping to walk into a new model experience. I was building a worship team based on works and not based on grace. When we talk about the work the Levites performed to prepare the sanctuary, we create a work-based environment that says if we do not put forth the work, God will not come through. That sounds profound, but it is not the demonstration of the New Covenant Grace. That puts God in a distant position from us. By doing so, we are waiting for God's arrival when, in reality, He's already present. We are no longer performing works for the setting of the place of worship. One of the New Covenant benefits is that God dwells on the inside of us. We know that God is omnipresent, but do we give credence to Him residing inside of us?

Responding to what we know causes us to focus on our behavior. We prioritize our works and our efforts as contributing to the Glory of God. The truth of the matter is, nothing we do contributes to the presence of God except being present. We are glory carriers. When a group of us come together, we unite the glory of God from inside us- moving ourselves out of the way. This occurs when we respond from belief rather than knowledge. What we know affects what we do, but what we believe affects who we are.

When approaching worship and the expressions of worship, we must respond from the position of rest. While on the cross, Christ's final words were "it is finished." (John 19:30) That means this is not a cause and effect movement. This is a respond by faith gesture. What we do is not for God to respond, but we do what we do because of the completed work. The works we do were in place for us before God formed this world. Our expressions of worship are in conjunction with that revelation. We express our reverence toward God as an act of faith in what is already done.

Some translations say, "Samuel served the LORD," and some say "ministered." The Hebrew translation for both words is sharath (H8334). Strong's definition states, "to attend as a menial or worshipper." This revelation changed my perspective of what it means to wait upon the Lord. Waiting is not a form of sitting until time passes. Waiting is engaging in worship that creates opportunities!

They that worship the Lord shall have renewed strength, and they will be able to mount on wings as eagles and soar!

Many churches are stuck because they position unequipped people who have no oil in leading the congregation into the presence of God.

In December 2016, I was in charge of administering a prayer service held at a church in Belleville, IL. As I was kneeling and the prayers were going forth, I had a vision of two streams of river merging into one. God spoke to me at that moment saying, "I am connecting two areas of giftings to work together as one in this season." I have never lost sight of that vision; however, until recently. I began to walk into a clearer understanding of what God was showing me.

A unique birthing takes place when we combine strong expressions of worship with solid intercession. When we worship God amid interceding, God begins to change the current of flow. Where we were worshipping or just making requests and declarations to God, we shifted into dialogue where God begins to speak back to us through prophetic utterance and song.

Many of us are not aware of the fact God sings to us. We don't often connect the lyrics that we bring spontaneously as a way of God getting our attention and pouring back into us. He not only speaks to us, but when miracles, signs and wonders begin to manifest before our eyes, that is God's ways of responding to our worship and intercession. It is God's follow up!

50

Chapter 7

SPIRIT AND TRUTH

In the beginning of the book of John, John talks about Christ being grace and truth. Later in the book, Christ reveals that worship is only valid through the Spirit and truth. Perhaps we have overthought this whole process. We have always described worship not being a place but a state of mind. But maybe worship is about positioning.

Jesus compares the two locations of worship as being natural, and we understand that Jesus's revelation eventually results in spiritual matters. Have you ever taken a moment to consider that grace and truth are equivalent to the Spirit and truth? In reality, our natural abilities cannot validate our salvation, so why would worship be something of the natural?

What Christ is saying is worship can only make a difference when you are in Him! That is when it becomes a lifestyle. The Words says it plainly: "It is no longer I that lives, but it is Christ who lives IN me (and through me)!" So, worship is all about positioning, but it is more about where you are positioned spiritually, fully submitted, and committed. It takes away the natural works of our hands and causes the validity of what we do to be manifested by Christ alone! He is our grace and truth, and He is the Spirit and truth!

Truth and Prophecy

God is spirit, and those who worship him must worship in spirit and truth.

John 4:24

Truth represents revelation or the revealed word, meaning we cannot truly worship God without a personal revelation of who God is. In First Corinthians 14:3 the Message translation says, "But when you proclaim truth in everyday speech, you're letting others in on the truth so that they can grow and be strong and experience his presence with you." The New International Version declares, "But the one who prophesies speaks to people for their strengthening, encouraging, and comfort." By this, we can say worshipping God in truth is allowing prophecy to come forth and true worship begins with prophecy.

Can we take a moment to review the definition of prophecy? My favorite defining of prophecy was given by Apostle John Eckhardt - to utter by inspiration of the Holy Spirit in a language that is known or unknown to the speaker. (Eckhardt God Still Speaks 2009) Keep in mind that worship and prophecy is the moment of releasing the word, not just receiving it. We understand that one who receives prophecy does not mean they immediately identify as a worshipper. I would dare to say this: to declare the truth of Jesus is in itself prophecy, for one cannot claim Jesus as Lord if it is not from God, Himself.

And I fell at his feet to worship him. And he said unto me, See thou do it not: I am thy fellow servant, and of thy brethren that have the testimony of Jesus: worship God: for the testimony of Jesus is the spirit of prophecy.

Revelation 19:10 KJV

If you want to be a sincere and effective witness of Jesus, prophesy. I remind you that the Spirit of God is on the inside of you. Tap into the realm of the Spirit. If you need help, worship God.

Worship opens the doors to the very secrets of God! If you want to know the mysteries of God concerning you, begin to worship. Whenever the kings inquired a word from the Lord, they would seek out a trustworthy prophet. You have read in some cases the prophet would request music to be played before they prophesy. Elisha was a great example:

> *So the king of Israel went with the king of Judah and the king of Edom. And when they had made a circuitous march of seven days, there was no water for the army or for the animals that followed them. Then the king of Israel said, "Alas! The LORD has called these three kings to give them into the hand of Moab." And Jehoshaphat said, "Is there no prophet of the LORD here, through whom we may inquire of the LORD?" Then one of the kings of Israel's servants answered, "Elisha the son of Shaphat is here, who poured water on the hands of Elijah."*
>
> *2 Kings 3:9-11*

It is important to note that true prophets are birthed and drawn through authentic worship. When there is an intense worship atmosphere, look around because you are more than likely going to find some prophets. Some may be aware of the office they walk in, and others may be in their discovery season.

> *Jehoshaphat said, "Yes, the LORD speaks through him."*
> *So the king of Israel, King Jehoshaphat of Judah, and the king of Edom went to consult with Elisha. "Why are you*

coming to me?" Elisha asked the king of Israel. "God to the pagan prophets of your father and mother!" But king Joram of Israel said, "No! For it was the LORD who called us three kings here - only to be defeated by the king of Moab!" Elisha replied, "As surely as the LORD Almighty lives, whom I serve, I wouldn't even bother with you except for my respect for King Jehoshaphat of Judah. Now bring me someone who can play the harp." While the harp was being played, the power of the LORD came upon Elisha, and he said, "This is what the LORD says: This dry valley will be filled with pools of water!"

2 Kings 3:12-16 NLT

Moreover David and the captains of the host separated to the service of the sons of Asaph, and of Heman, and of Jeduthun, who should prophesy with harps, with psalteries, and with cymbals: and the number of the workmen according to their service was: of the sons of Asaph, Zaccur, and Joseph, and Nethaniah, and Asarelah, the sons of Asaph under the hands of Asaph, which prophesied according to the order of the king. Of Jeduthun: the sons of Jeduthun; Gedaliah, and Zeri, and Jeshaiah, Hashabiah, and Mattithiah, six, under the hands of their father Jeduthun, who prophesied with a harp, to give thanks and to praise the LORD. Of Heman:

the sons of Heman: Bukkiah, Mattaniah, Uzziel, Shebuel, and Jerimoth, Hananiah, Hanani, Eliathah, Giddalti, and Romamtiezer, Joshbehashah, Mallothi, Hothir, and Mahazioth: All these were the sons of Heman the king's seer in the words of God, to lift up the horn. And God gave to Heman fourteen sons and three daughters. All these were under the hands of their father for song in the house of the LORD, with cymbals, psalteries, and harps, for the service of the house of God, according to the king's order to Asaph, Jeduthun, and Heman.

1 Chronicles 25:1-6 KJV

I want to break down a few of the names because I believe they will enlighten you.

Asaph

The meaning of the name Asaph is "gatherer." Asaph was a chief Levite musician who oversaw his sons. The verse said they would prophesy according to the king's order. Some translations state "the hand of the king." which interprets as power, strength, portion or share. (Strong's Hebrew Lexicon). This family released God's messages through worship by way of delegated authority. Authentic expressions of worship gather people from all cultures and backgrounds. This anointing is especially necessary so that the word of God can be released. Some have the gift to unite people through worship - not for entertainment, but for creating a dialogue with God. Worship leaders are anointed to release the song of the Lord through the power, strength and portion of God. God empowers us and He strengthens us to speak on his behalf.

The Sons of Asaph

Zaccur means "mindful." Sometimes we need reminding that God is mindful of us. What He does for us and what He says to us is always for our best interest. God is so mindful of us that He takes time to dwell with us and speak to us. When we engage in expressive worship, God makes a personal effort to see about us. He speaks over us, and He sings over us.

The second son's name was Joseph, meaning, "Jehovah has added." God is a God of multiplication. When we engage in worship, what He speaks to us adds to us. It adds to our calling; it adds to our purpose and identity; it adds to our weaponry; it adds to our stamina in the spirit! God is continuously adding to us!

The third son's name mentioned was Nethaniah. His same carries the meaning "Given of Jehovah." It is evident that God desires to give. His whole nature is about giving.

My wife and I were in a two-bedroom apartment. It was our second apartment together. It was a slight upgrade from the first. We lived in a unit where a washer and dryer hookup were provided. We had an old stacker that we bought from a resale appliance store. It was working for a while, but eventually, it went out. Just like most inconvenient situations, it went out during the time we had no money to repair or replace the unit. One night my wife requested that we worshipped together. We moved the couch out of the way, turned on something from Pandora Music, and worshipped God. At that moment, we didn't ask anything from God even though we had needs. We acknowledged God for who He was and is, then basked in His presence. The next day, a close family member handed us a pamphlet to my wife and me. It was a picture of our brand-new washer and dryer with a warranty. That was a testimony to prove that when we deny ourselves in worship, God will open up supernatural doors of favor.

> *But seek ye first the kingdom of God, and his righteousness; and all these things shall be added unto you.*
>
> *Matthew 6:33 KJV*

The fourth son of Asaph was Asar'elah. His name meant "God holds." Worship establishes God's control in our life. God secures our future, purpose, and plans. Worship also creates a space that allows God to hold us. Have you ever faced a situation so dense and tough where all you could was go to God? Sometimes you don't have the strength to say a word, but at that moment, God comes in and comforts you.

We can all agree that when we gather for worship, God confirms that He is mindful of us; He adds to us, gives to us, and will continue to hold us.

What is man, that thou art mindful of him? and the son of man, that thou visitest him?

Psalm 8:4 KJV

The LORD hath been mindful of us: he will bless us; he will bless the house of Israel; he will bless the house of Aaron.

Psalm 115:12 KJV

And this is the record, that God hath given to us eternal life, and this life is in his Son.

1 John 5:11 KJV

Blessed be the Lord, who daily loadeth us with benefits, even the God of our salvation. Selah.

Psalm 68:19 KJV

Worship not only opens doors for the favor and mysteries of God, but it also provides a way for transformation! When Samuel approached Saul, one of the first instructions given to him was to meet a company of prophets on the way up a hill. The prophets were not just standing around looking for a man to prophesy to, but they were engaged in worship. Through their participation, they created such an atmosphere that it pulled Saul, who was not a prophet, into the dimension of prophecy, even to the point where others who knew Saul questioned if he was a prophet.

When you arrive at Gibeah of God, where the garrison of the Philistines is located, you will meet a band of prophets coming down from the place of worship. They will be playing a harp, a tambourine, a flute, and a lyre, and they will be prophesying. At that time the Spirit of the LORD will come powerfully upon you, and you will prophesy with them. You will be changed into a different person.

1 Samuel 10:5-6

When Saul and his servant arrived at Gibeah, they saw a group of prophets coming toward them. Then the Spirit of God came powerfully upon Saul, and he, too, began to prophesy. When those who knew Saul heard about it, they exclaimed, "What? Is even Saul a prophet? How did the son of Kish become a prophet?"

1 Samuel 10:10-11

This is how strong the spirit of prophecy becomes. When you have a group of prophets who worship, it produces an atmosphere that influences everyone present. Yes - even an unbeliever.

Even so, if unbelievers or people who don't understand these things come into your church meeting and hear everyone speaking in an unknown language, they will think you are crazy. But if all of you are prophesying, and unbelievers or people who don't understand these things come into your meeting, they will be convicted of sin and judged by what you say. As they listen, their secret thoughts will be exposed, and they will fall to their knees and worship God, declaring, "God is truly here among you."

1 Corinthians 14:23-25

I perceive in the Spirit that we are about to witness a preeminent breakout of atmosphere-shifting worship. This vast shift will not be just a movement, but it will introduce a new reality of what should consist of in our gatherings. I prophesy that there will be many converted individuals from other religions that will come to know God through authentic worship. I believe God is going to position mature and genuine prophets in the area of worship that will guide and equip others to follow heaven's blueprint for glory encounters.

Chapter 8

WORSHIP AND HEAVEN

If you want to experience heaven, begin to worship and stop inquiring about death!

Worship creates a dwelling place for the presence of God. The footstool of God is the earth, which means the earth should be filled with not just the glory of God but our worship as well. As we create an atmosphere of worship in the earth, we make room for God to speak to us corporately. The earth is also, prophetically speaking, our hearts, and this body. When we sing and make music with all our soul (see Psalm 108:1) we are indicating that we are using every bit of our mind, will, and emotions to produce a sound that will set the tone for heaven to make its entrance.

Yet you are holy, enthroned on the praises of Israel.

Psalm 22:3

This is what the LORD says: "Heaven is my throne, and the earth is my footstool. Could you build me a temple as good as that? Could you build me such a resting place?"

Isaiah 66:1

Worship creates the atmosphere of heaven. The atmosphere is not duplicate to or similar to heaven; it is heaven. When something is similar, there are distinct characteristics that differentiate the two. When we describe the atmosphere of worship as the atmosphere of heaven, there is no difference.

When we attempt to describe heaven, we are confident that some things are not present. Such things as sickness, lack, depression, fear, etc. do not exist in heaven. In connection to scripture, these things do not exist in the Kingdom of heaven. When we boldly declare, "Your Kingdom come, Your will be done," we are creating a direct right of access for heaven to impact the earth. Many times in the New Testament, God performed great movements by way of worship and intercession. Worship is an atmosphere purifier. It is a force that causes forces unseen to align with the proper settings of Heaven so that God can do what He does best.

...your kingdom come, your will be done, on earth as it is in heaven.

Matthew 6:10 NIV

Heal the sick, and tell them, 'The Kingdom of God is near you now.'

Luke 10:9

I heard a loud shout from the throne, saying, "Look, God's home is now among his people! He will live them, and they will be his people. God himself will be with them. He will wipe every tear from their eyes, and there will be no more death or sorrow or crying or pain. All these things are gone forever."

Revelation 21:3-4

I am head of the intercession team at the church I attend, Redeemers House of Worship, where I server as seer. We typically pray Sunday mornings before worship service as a way to set the tone for the day. One morning as we were praying, God began releasing fresh wisdom. God shared, "we must secure what I have established." When we intercede and even when worship, we are securing the will of God on the earth; the promises of God, and the very thing God established by way of His word. As we worship God, we begin to secure the atmosphere so that Heaven can make impact.

We must not be ignorant of unseen demonic activity that is always around, waiting for an opening to mess up God's plan or create a detour to delay the move of God. Our worship engages in the world of unseen and calls to attention angels that are waiting to move on our behalf. It activates a realm of security so that the King has free range.

In 2008, I was a freshman attending the University of Illinois, Springfield. The area would typically be slow with not much activity going on as we were near the cornfields right before you enter into the busy city of Springfield. This day was different. I was very annoyed because on every corner, you saw several police cars. They were hidden in the streets and on the highway, leaving not one area unsecured. Someone reminded me that President Barak Obama was arranged to be in town. Everything made sense. The premises needed proper securing for the President's arrival. Even though he was going to be at one location, they not only had to secure the pathway that he was going to travel, but they had to have security in places miles from the meeting place.

Our worship is nothing short of that example. It has an even more significant impact. Our worship creates a place where it searches for every wrong, every lack, and it corrects it so that our King can make His entrance. Do not take your worship lightly! It does more than we can see with the natural eye. We must pray the prayer of Elisha over worship teams, and even our congregation, that God opens our eyes to the things that we cannot see.

> *"Don't be afraid!" Elisha told him. "For there are more on our side than on theirs!" Then Elisha prayed, "O LORD, open his eyes and let him see!" The LORD opened the young man's eyes, and when he looked up, he saw that the hillside around Elisha was filled with horses and chariots of fire."*
>
> *2 Kings 6:16-17*

What a powerful revelation! Our worship reminds us that we are not alone at that very moment. We have a host of angel armies surrounding us in the unseen dimension, ready to engage in warfare! It gets better!

> *As the Aramean army advanced toward him, Elisha prayed, "O LORD, please make them blind." So the LORD struck them with blindness as Elisha had asked.*
>
> *2 Kings 6:18*

God is ready to blind our enemies by the activating of our worship! Our worship blinds sickness itself and lack so that it has no power in the space in which we dwell. There is a spirit of Elisha in worship that activates the ability to see what is unseen as well as blind what comes against us!

Chapter 9

THE ATTACK ON WORSHIP

When we consider all the great movements of God, no doubt worship was involved. What we saw was the result of authentic worship, stemmed from the heart and not our hands. When we are engaged in the act of entertainment, we block the full encounter of God. We are covered in falsehood.

During the time I was serving at my grandparents' church, I would spend time on Saturdays praying alone. During one of those sessions, God began to release the words "Spirit of Elijah." I began to ask the question, "Why Elijah?" Out of ignorance and excitement, my response was "because I wasn't afraid to ask for the double portion." I thought I was the business. After studying the scriptures more, I then discovered how far from accurate I was indeed. I mistook that thought by Elisha, not Elijah. I was back to square one. It wasn't until recently, I was reading a book, Who's Who in the Bible, and out of curiosity, I looked up Elijah and was blown away. Here is a piece from the book.

"As the Baal worship of Tyre made inroads into Israel through Jezebel, Elijah was sent to check its spread by emphasizing again that Israel's God was the only God of the whole earth. He began a vital work that was continued by Jehu, who slaughtered many of the Baal worshipers among Israel's leaders. Elijah's specific mission was to destroy heathen worship to spare Israel, thus preparing the way for the prophets who were to follow in his spirit." (Comfort & Elwell The Complete Book of Who's Who in the Bible 2014)

Then Jehu called a meeting of all the people of the city and said to them, "Ahab's worship of Baal was nothing compared to the way I will worship him! Therefore, summon all the prophets and worshipers of Baal, and call together all his priests. See to it that every one of them comes, for I am going to offer a great sacrifice to Baal. Anyone who fails to come will be put to death." But Jehu's cunning plan was to destroy all the worshipers of Baal.

Then Jehu ordered, "Prepare a solemn assembly to worship Baal!" So they did. He sent messengers throughout all Israel summoning those who worshiped

Baal. They all came - not a single one remained behind - and they filled the temple of Baal from one end to the other. And Jehu instructed the keeper of the wardrobe, "Be sure that every worshiper of Baal wear one of these robes." So robes were given to them.

Then Jehu went into the temple of Baal with Jehonadab son of Recab. Jehu said to the worshipers of Baal, "Make sure no one worships the LORD is here - only those who worship Baal." So they were all inside the temple to offer sacrifices and burnt offerings. Now Jehu had stationed eighty of his men outside the building and had warned them, "If you let anyone escape, you will pay for it with your own life."

As soon as Jehu had finished sacrificing the burnt offering, he commanded his guards and officers, "Go in and kill all of them. Don't let a single one escape!" So they killed them all with their swords, and the guards and officers dragged their bodies outside. Then Jehu's men went into the innermost fortress of the temple of Baal. They dragged out the sacred pillar used in the worship of Baal and burned it. They smashed the sacred pillar and wrecked the temple of Baal, converting it into a public toilet, as it remains to this day. In this way, Jehu destroyed every trace of Baal worship from Israel.

2 Kings 10:18-28

I have always had a strong passion for worship. I become vexed in my spirit every time I am faced with a spirit of entertainment, a false spirit of worship, and as I have discovered, Baal worship. When we find ourselves living for anything other than God, we lead ourselves into bondage rather than freedom. We find ourselves enslaved rather than sonship.

We can have so many legitimate motives behind our worship, but I believe it is time to be restored into the actual reality of worship. That is when we live beyond the expressions of worship and start living from the heart. We must allow our obedience to God be the center of our daily works. Every time I worship, I find myself going into ample space. A space of no boundaries or limitations. An area of real transparency and nakedness. A space where you don't have to hide. It is time for God to rip the veil in our lives that separate us from Him.

And I am convinced that nothing can ever separate us from God's love. Neither death nor life, neither angels nor demons, neither our fears for today nor our worries about tomorrow - not even the powers of hell can separate us from God's love. No power in the sky above or in the earth below - indeed, nothing in all creation will ever be able to separate us from the love of God that is revealed in Christ Jesus our Lord.

Romans 8:38-39

Some of the areas we can go wrong during worship: we aim to minister to the congregation rather than to God, and we place more emphasis on the natural sound rather than the moment. When there is authentic worship, you don't have to worry about leaving people behind. It is all about the atmosphere. When the atmosphere is right, everyone's heart is on one accord. Mighty things take place where there is unity. Unity should not be on the agenda created by man, but it should be in the unity of the Holy Spirit.

We must also consider the songs that we sing. Some songs that were written by others were good for a specific time and purpose. Prophetic worship, or spontaneous worship, may require a new song on the spot. We do this by drawing from the Holy Spirit and not pulling from our understanding. As a worship leader, I see a more excellent response in corporate worship when I sing the song of the Lord rather than one that everyone knows. That is key because we minister from what we need rather than what we know.

Sing a new song of praise to him; play skillfully on the harp and sing with joy.

Psalm 33:3

He put a new song in my mouth, a hymn of praise to our God. Many will see and fear the LORD and put their trust in him.

Psalm 40:3 NIV

And they sang a new song with these words: "You are worthy to take the scroll and break its seals and open it. For you were slaughtered, and your blood has ransomed people for God from every tribe and language and people and nation."

Revelation 5:9

But God hath revealed them unto us by his Spirit: for the Spirit searcheth all things, yea, the deep things of God.

2 Corinthians 2:10 KJV

Singing a new song pulls on everyone, not just the psalmists. Everyone that is ministering through expressions of worship is on one accord with the Spirit. Just as the scriptures declare, the ushering of a new song can also be delivered by the musicians. I remind you of the family of Asaph and how they were responsible for prophesying on behalf of the king through instruments.

There needs to be an understanding that skilled does not mean anointed. You have many who are competent but do not carry the anointing. That does not mean that there is no calling on their life. The spirit through which they play may be their own and not the Spirit God. You then have the remnant of those who are anointed but not skilled. There are faithful servants who occupy the space because of need and passion. I am sure everyone knows at least one person who has the heart and desire to sing but cannot hold a note, yet the atmosphere shifts when they open up their mouth.

There must be a healthy balance of skill and anointing. I believe that every gift must go through training and development. I am also convinced that during the process of technical development, there must be a personal interest in the giver of the gift. It is essential to take time to understand the why of the gift.

Last but not least, we need to return to God as the center of our worship. God will not share the glory with anyone or anything. God is incapable of competing. To compete with something or someone means to measure both strengths and weaknesses against another. God has no defects. He is incomparable.

"I am the LORD; that is my name! I will not give my glory to anyone else, nor share my praise with carved idols."

Isaiah 42:8

The Hebrew word for glory translates as honor, reverence, and my favorite, reputation. God boldly states that he will not share His reputation of all-powerful, all-knowing, ever-present with anyone or anything. The adoration that we give during worship, and our daily living goes to God and God alone.

In First Samuel, the Philistines brought the ark of God into the house of Dagon. When they returned the next morning, they, Dagon, the idol that was sitting next to the ark of God, was found face down on the ground. They placed Dagon back in place, but the following morning, Dagon was found once again on the ground. This time, however, the head and hands of Dagon were cut off from the rest of its body.

After the Philistines captured the Ark of God, they took it from the battleground at Ebenezer to the town of Ashdod. They carried the Ark of God into the temple of Dagon and placed it beside an idol of Dagon. But when the citizens of Ashdod went to see it the next morning, Dagon had fallen with his face to the ground in front of the Ark of the LORD! So they took Dagon and put him in his place again. But the next morning the same thing happened -

Dagon had fallen face down before the Ark of the LORD again. This time his head and hands had broken off and were lying in the doorway. Only the trunk of his body was left intact.

1 Samuel 5:1-4

You adapt to the image of who and what you worship. The danger of worshipping idols is that we become what we worship - having eyes but cannot see; having ears but cannot hear; having mouths but cannot speak. When we worship God, our spirits are quickened into life, and we are able to breathe again.

Why let the nations say, "Where is their God?" Our God is in the heavens, and he does as he wishes. Their idols are merely things of silver and gold, shaped by human hands. They have mouths but cannot speak, and eyes but see. They have ears but cannot hear, and noses but cannot smell. They have hands but cannot feel, and feet but cannot walk, and throats but cannot make a sound. And those who make idols are just like them, as are all who trust in them.

Psalm 115:2-8

God gives us life. Where we are depleted, He comes to refresh. What we have lost, God can restore. What has died, He can revive.

Conclusion

THE INVITATION

I believe it is time for us as a nation to repent. We have placed all things concerning creation upon a pedestal. We have put it in a place where God belongs. Although repentance requires acknowledgment of where we are, we must know that true repentance is not a confession; it is to change what we are doing. Read the following prayer from the heart and allow God to transform you. Please know that the process of change for some does not happen overnight. As long as you are willing to go through the process, I can assure you that God will be with you every step of the way.

Dear God,

I acknowledge that my heart has been in the wrong place. I took Your creation and put it in a place where You belong. I worship You as my Creator and King. More importantly, I worship You as the ultimate Father. I have filled my heart with what I thought was important, pushing myself far from the truth. Even though I deserve to be thrown aside and forgotten, You have yet to give up on me. You have never left me nor forsaken me.

I stand to agree that You are the one true God who is worthy of honor, glory, and praise. Today, I decided to lay down my idols. Today, I decided to honor You. At this moment, I give You my heart, my plans, my desires in exchange for Yours. I know You will never lead me astray, but You will lead me to victory. I thank You for Your Son, Jesus Christ. It is by His works alone that I can have this relationship with You, God. I believe that the work He did on the cross was for my redemption. It was for me to be reconciled back to You. I receive the new mindset of Christ. I know that this change may not be easy, but with the partnering of Your Spirit, I know that my transformation is inevitable. I will keep my eyes on You, Father, and be transformed into the image of Your Son, Jesus Christ.

Amen

RESOURCES

Comfort, Philip Wesley., and Walter A. Elwell. The Complete Book of Whos Who in the Bible. Castle Books, 2014.

Eckhardt, John. God Still Speaks. Charisma House, 2009.

"H2139 - Zakkuwr - Strong's Hebrew Lexicon (KJV)." Blue Letter Bible, www.blueletterbible.org/lang/lexicon/lexicon.cfm?strongs=H2139.

"H3084 - Yĕhowceph - Strong's Hebrew Lexicon (KJV)." Blue Letter Bible, www.blueletterbible.org/lang/lexicon/lexicon.cfm?strongs=H3084.

"H3322 - Yatsag - Strong's Hebrew Lexicon (KJV)." Blue Letter Bible, www.blueletterbible.org/lang/lexicon/lexicon.cfm?strongs=H3322.

"H3519 - Kabowd - Strong's Hebrew Lexicon (KJV)." Blue Letter Bible, www.blueletterbible.org/lang/lexicon/lexicon.cfm?Strongs=H3519&t=KJV.

"H4503 - Minchah - Strong's Hebrew Lexicon (KJV)." Blue Letter Bible, www.blueletterbible.org/lang/lexicon/lexicon.cfm?strongs=H4503.

"H4672 - Matsa' - Strong's Hebrew Lexicon (KJV)." Blue Letter Bible, www.blueletterbible.org/lang/lexicon/lexicon.cfm?strongs=H4672.

"H5418 - Nĕthanyah - Strong's Hebrew Lexicon (KJV)." Blue Letter Bible, www.blueletterbible.org/lang/lexicon/lexicon.cfm?strongs=H5418.

"H623 - 'Acaph - Strong's Hebrew Lexicon (KJV)." Blue Letter Bible, www.blueletterbible.org/lang/lexicon/lexicon.cfm?strongs=H623.

"H7126 - Qarab - Strong's Hebrew Lexicon (KJV)." Blue Letter Bible, www.blueletterbible.org/lang/lexicon/lexicon.cfm?strongs=H7126.

"H8334 - Sharath - Strong's Hebrew Lexicon (KJV)." Blue Letter Bible, www.blueletterbible.org/lang/lexicon/lexicon.cfm?Strongs=H8334&t=KJV.

"H841 - 'Asar'elah - Strong's Hebrew Lexicon (KJV)." Blue Letter Bible, www.blueletterbible.org/lang/lexicon/lexicon.cfm?strongs=H841.

WHAT IS LSM-REAL

If you are anything like me, then you know what feels like to be in a position where you are unsure if you are hearing from God. You might have had the unction from the Holy Spirit, leading you to do or say something, but you don't find out until it is almost too late. I am sure many of us can relate to that. With so many mentors and coaches in the world, you wonder why you have not connected with anyone. You wonder why you feel so... alone.

I have battled in my journey for quite some time with understanding God's path for my life. I began to understand that God has been speaking to me the whole time- I was simply ignorant to His channel of communication to me. It is an uneasy feeling.

I, along with my wife, Airlia Salley are kingdom trailblazers in the STL Region. God began to open our eyes to understanding why we faced the challenges that we did when it came to not just knowing our purpose but also functioning in our purpose. We understand what it is like to deal with the common struggles of becoming from identity crisis to rejection. Unfortunately we cannot help you evade the challenges of discovering who you are, however, our desire is to guide every step we can!

Lawrence Salley Ministries is a mentoring guide that walks you through unveiling God's voice in your life, focusing on Worship, Writing and Intercession. We also focus on the balance of God's involvement in every area of life.

Come let us Discover Together.

CONNECT WITH THE AUTHOR

89

Facebook: WWW.FACEBOOK.COM/LSMREAL

Email: LSMREAL@GMAIL.COM

Website: WWW.LSMREAL.COM